Joseph Haydn
(1732–1809)

Sonatas

Sonates

Sonaten

I

for piano · pour piano · für Klavier

Urtext

K 121

INDEX

I

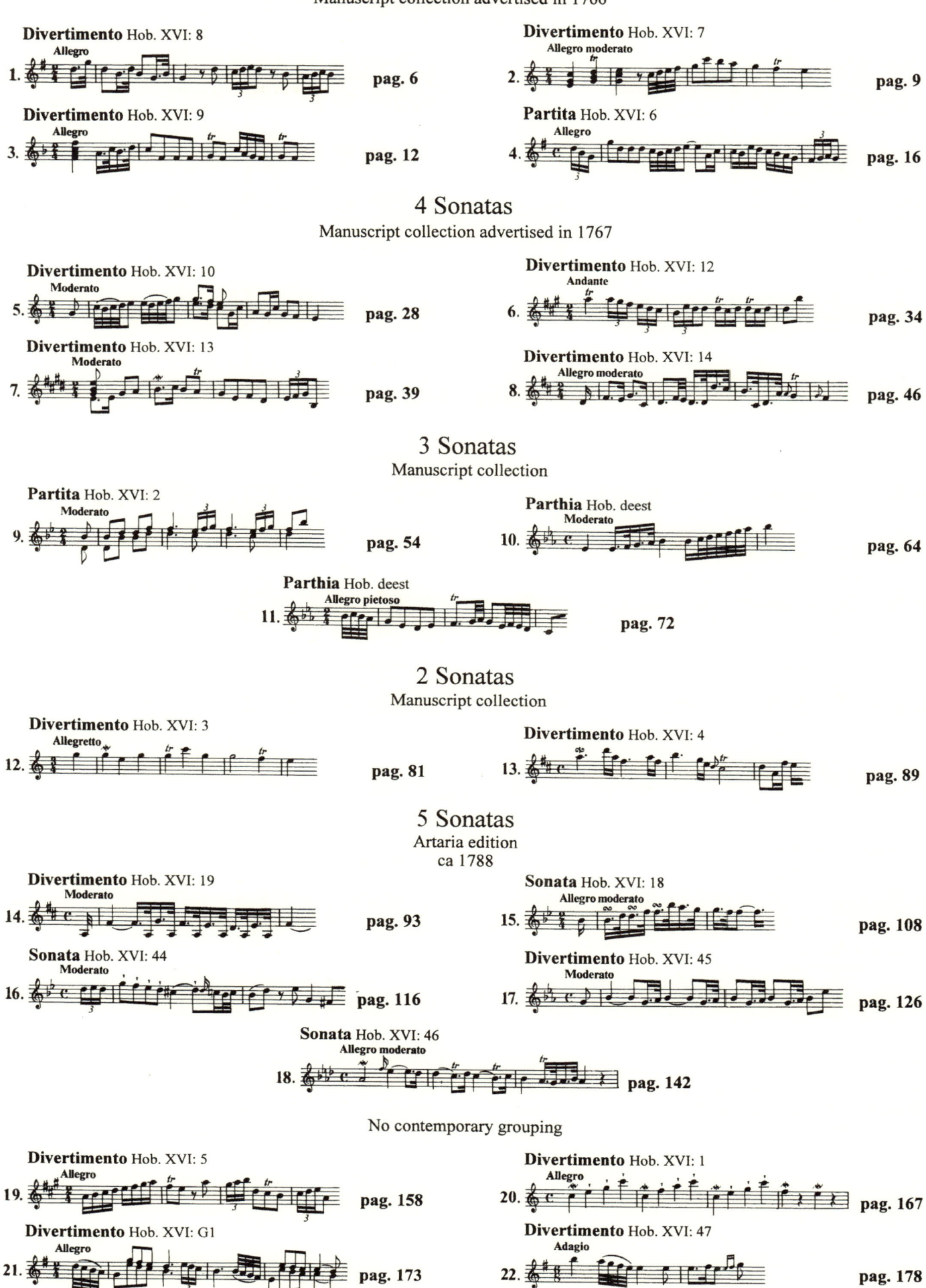

INDEX
II

6 Sonate („Esterházy" Sonate), 1774

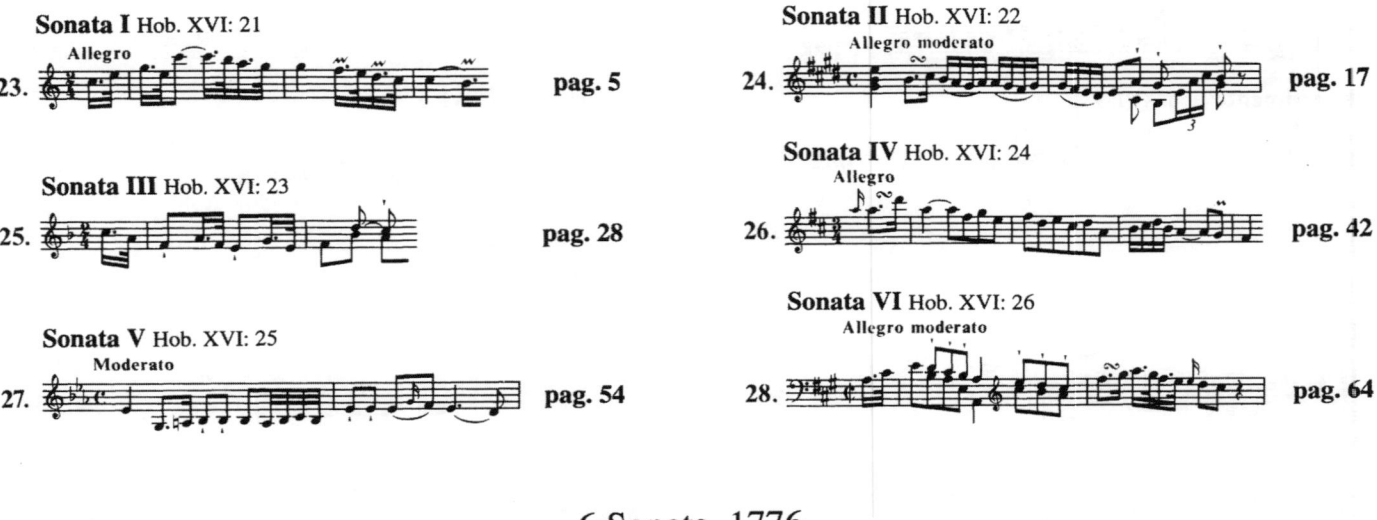

6 Sonate, 1776

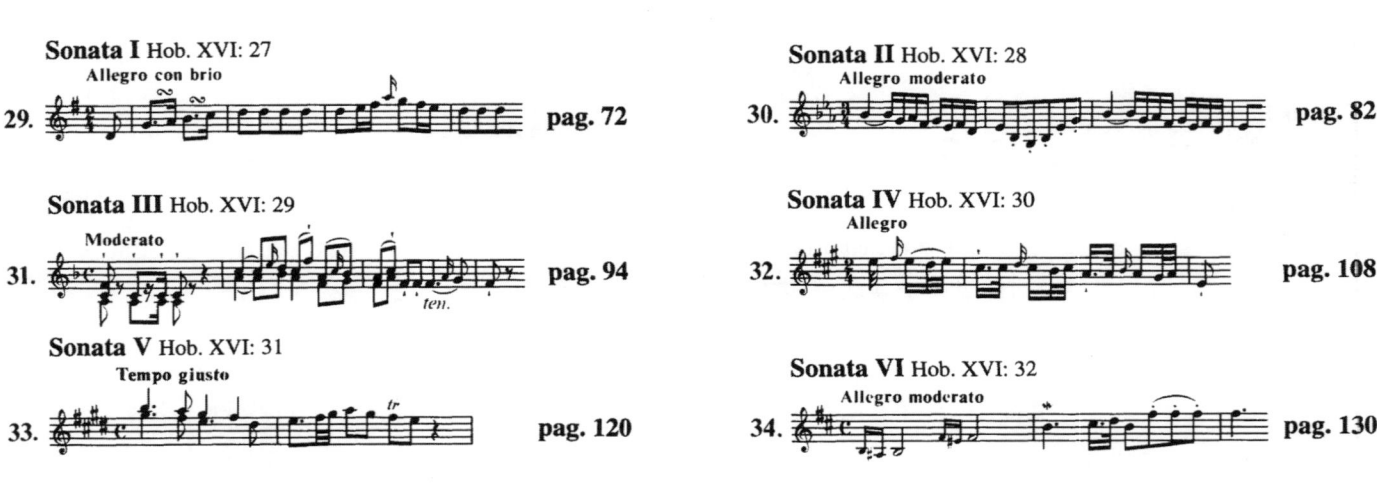

6 Sonate („Auenbrugger" Sonate), 1780

INDEX

III

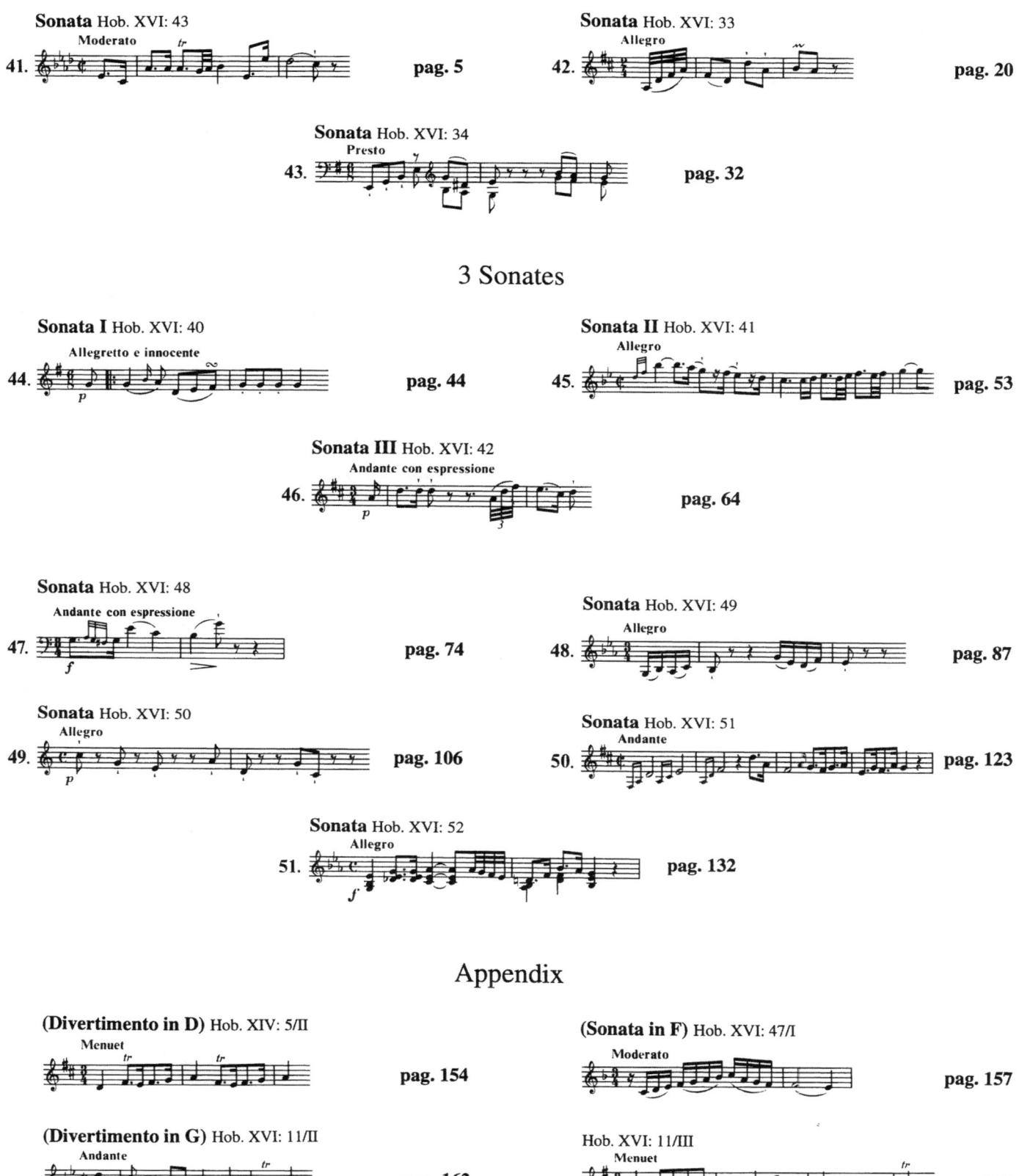

4 Sonatas
Manuscript collection advertised in 1766

Divertimento

Hob. XVI: 8

Divertimento

Divertimento

Menuet da Capo

Scherzo

Partita

Hob. XVI: 6

Minuet da Capo

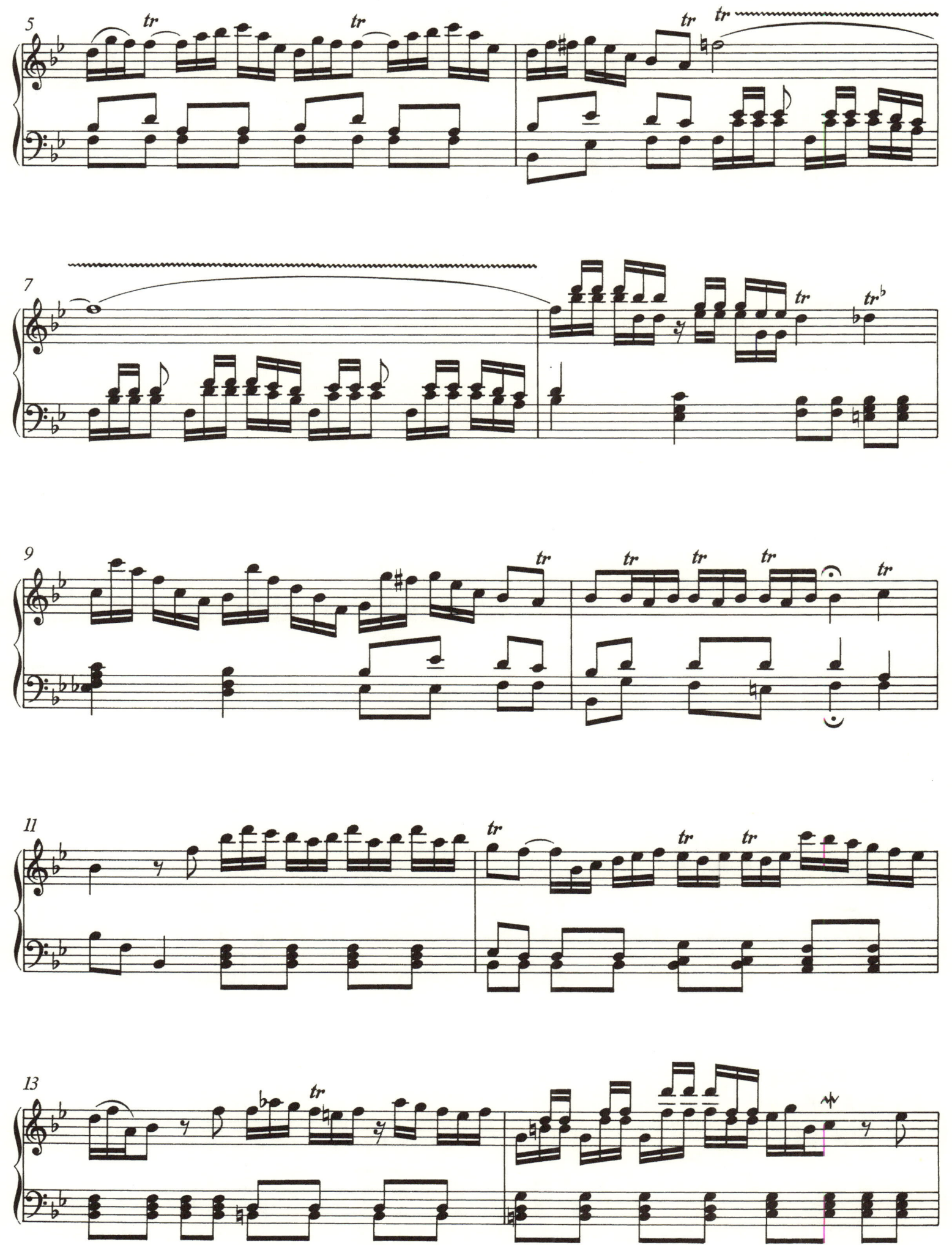

Finale
Allegro molto

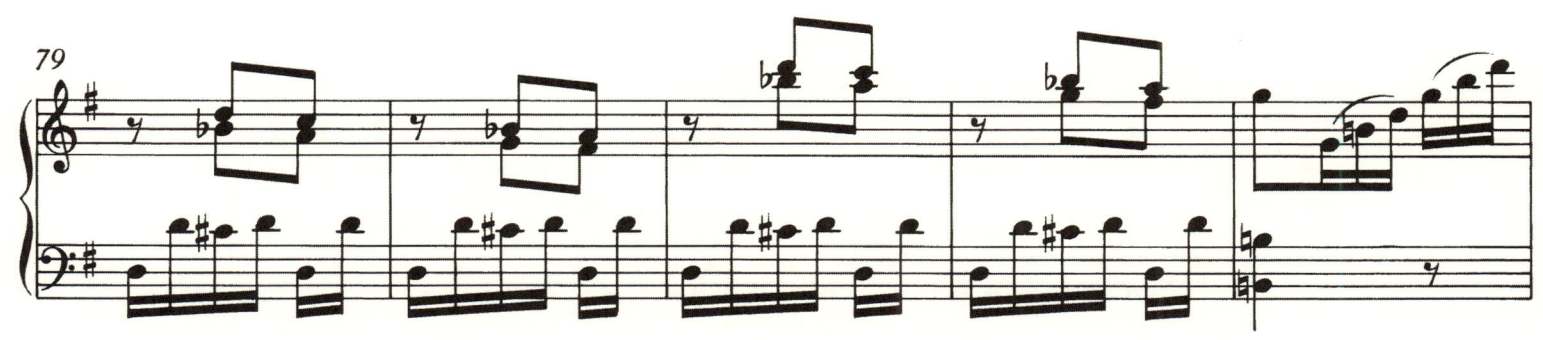

4 Sonatas
Manuscript collection advertised in 1767

Divertimento

Hob. XVI: 10

Finale
Presto

Divertimento

Hob. XVI: 12

Divertimento

Hob. XVI: 13

Divertimento

Hob. XVI: 14

Allegro moderato

Menuet

3 Sonatas
Manuscript collection

Partita

Hob. XVI: 2

Menuet

K 121

Parthia

Menuetto

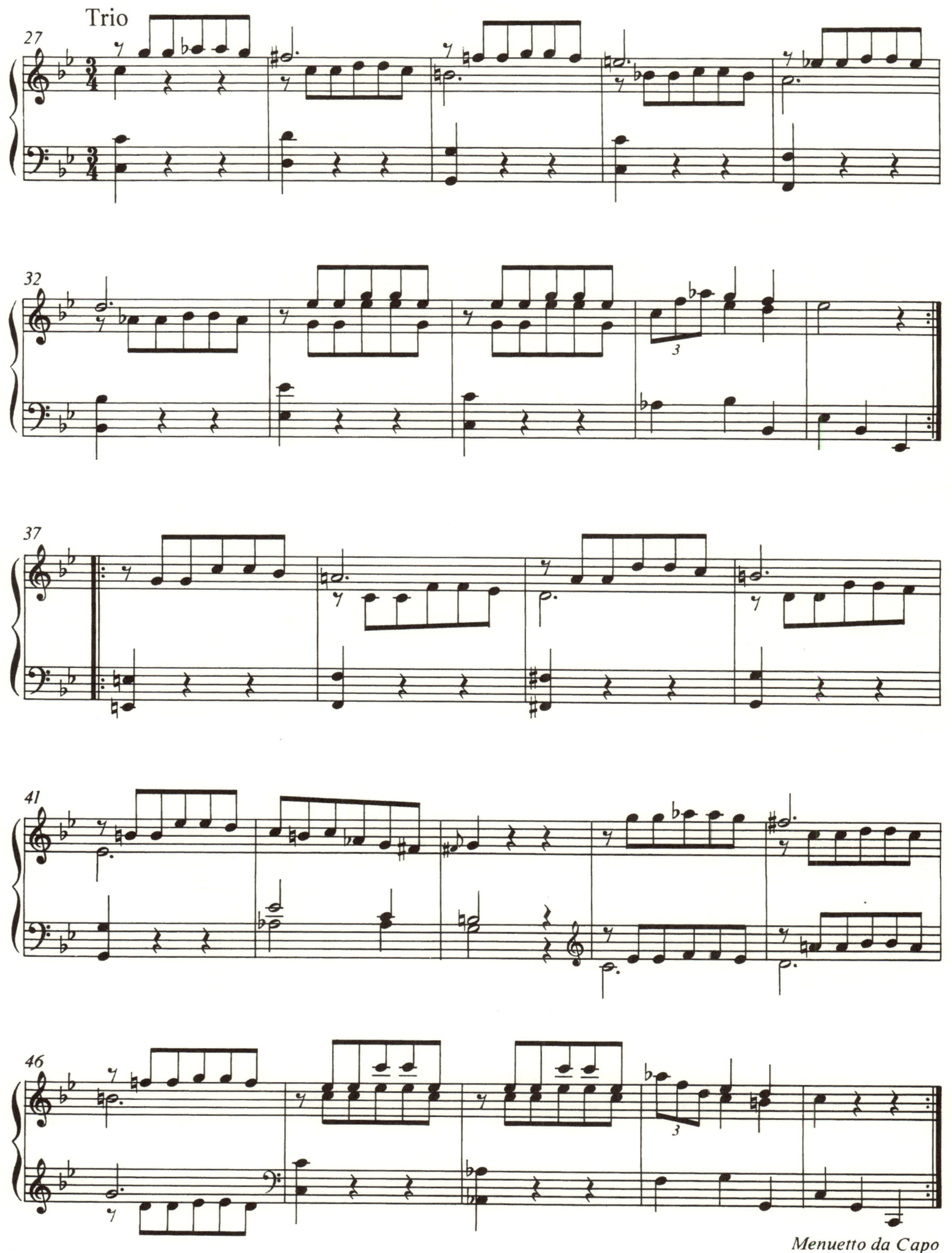

Parthia

Menuetto

K 121

2 Sonatas
Manuscript collection

Divertimento

Hob. XVI: 3

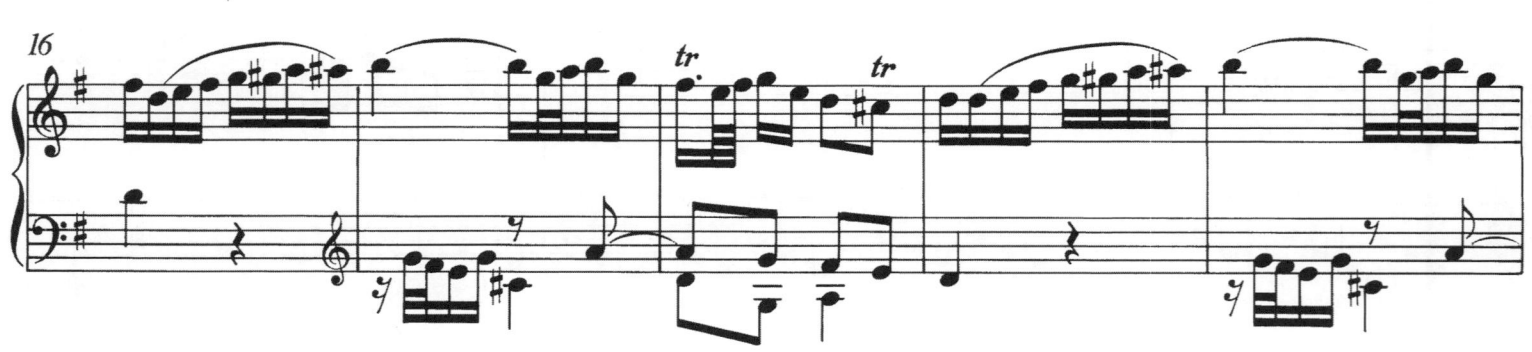

Trio

Menuet da Capo

Divertimento

Hob. XVI: 4

Menuetto da Capo

5 Sonatas
Artaria edition ca 1788

Divertimento

Hob. XVI: 19
1767

Moderato

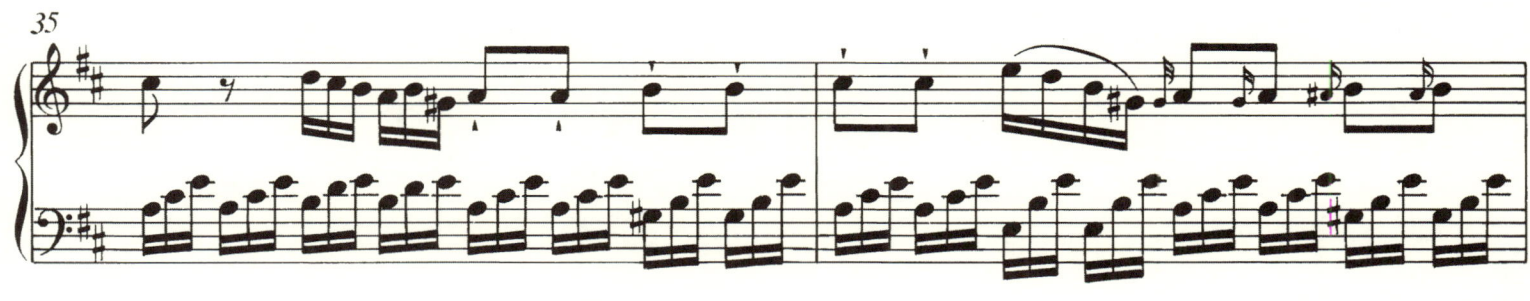

Sonata

Hob. XVI: 18

Sonata

Hob. XVI: 44

16. Moderato

Divertimento

Hob. XVI: 45
1766

128

Finale
Allegro di molto

Sonata

Allegro moderato

Hob. XVI: 46

18.

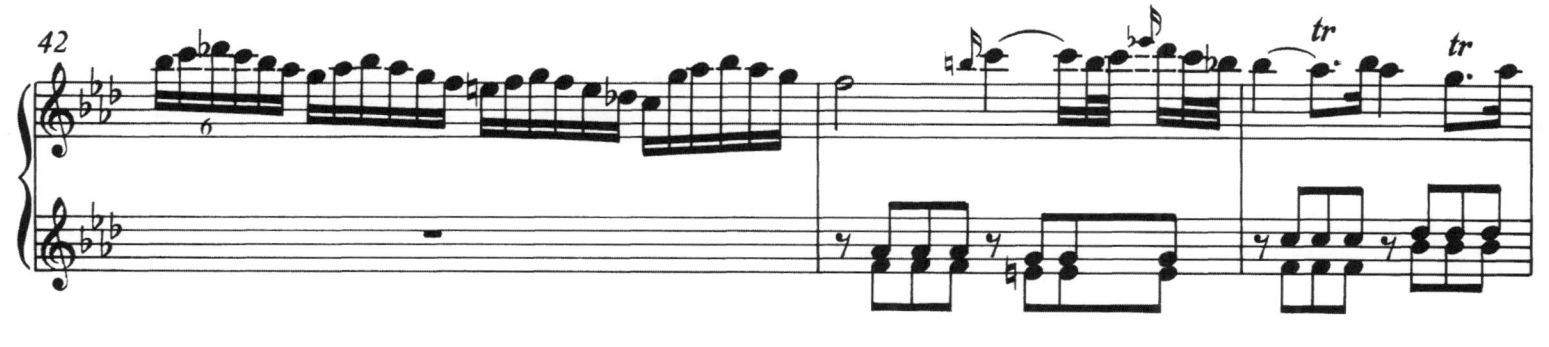

K 121

Finale
Presto

No contemporary grouping

Divertimento

Hob. XVI: 5

Divertimento

Hob. XVI: 1

20. Allegro

Divertimento

Hob. XVI: G1

Finale
Presto

Da Capo al Segno

Divertimento

Hob. XVI: 47

Adagio

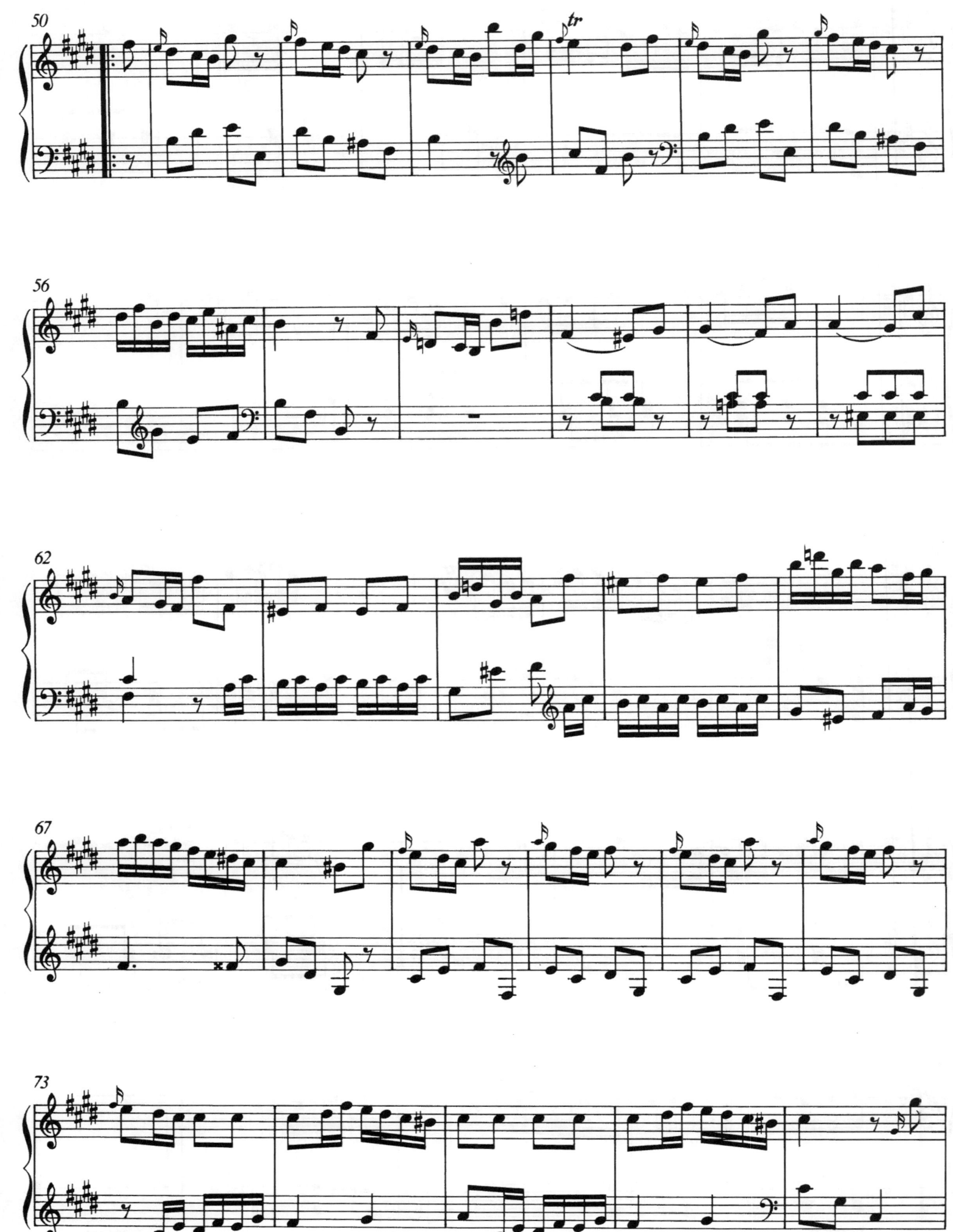

Finale
Tempo di Menuet

 **MUSICA PIANO**

OVER 25.000 PAGES OF PIANO MUSIC SHEETS ONLINE

Bach, Beethoven, Brahms, Chopin, Czerny, Debussy, Gershwin, Dvořák, Grieg, Haydn, Joplin, Lyadov, Mendelssohn-Bartholdy, Mozart, Mussorgsky, Purcell, Schubert, Schumann, Scriabin, Tchaikovsky and many more

KÖNEMANN

© 2018 koenemann.com GmbH
www.koenemann.com

Editor: Miklós Dolinszky
Responsible co-editor: István Máriássy
Technical editor: Dezső Varga
Engraved by Kottamester Bt., Budapest

ISBN 978-3-7419-1481-2

Printed in China by Reliance Printing